Our Holidays

Sometimes, even as you live a moment, you know it will become a favorite memory. Because certain moments have a magic to them. They glow from the inside out. They shine just a bit more brightly.

The holidays are full of times like these—from the joyful rituals and the cherished traditions to the loving gestures and the acts of generosity.

Capture the brightest moments of your holidays here. Write them down together, and remember them for always... year after shining year.

The most
beautiful things...
are memories
and moments.

ALEK WEK

YEAR:

THIS HOLIDAY SEASON

Our special events, outings, gatherings & celebrations

DATE

What we did:

What we want to remember:

DATE

What we did:

What we want to remember:

DATE

What we did:

What we want to remember:

DATE

What we did:

What we want to remember:

Shared reflections

A favorite moment of holiday togetherness:

A person it was really special to hear from or see this holiday:

An activity that brought us a lot of shared joy:

An aspect of holiday spirit we want to try to carry into the new year:

Highlights

These were some of the season's brightest moments:

Inspire, share love, join hands, open hearts. We are here for each other.

LAUREL BURCH

YEAR:

THIS HOLIDAY SEASON

Our special events, outings, gatherings & celebrations

DATE

What we did:

What we want to remember:

DATE

What we did:

What we want to remember:

DATE

What we did:

What we want to remember:

DATE

What we did:

What we want to remember:

Shared reflections

The sweetest surprise of the season was:

Something we feel particularly grateful for this holiday:

A moment of laughter we want to remember:

Some new things we want to do or try together this coming year:

Highlights

These were some of the season's brightest moments:

The joy that you give to others is the joy that comes back to you.

MARGARET E. SANGSTER

YEAR:

THIS HOLIDAY SEASON

Our special events, outings, gatherings & celebrations

DATE

What we did:

What we want to remember:

DATE

What we did:

What we want to remember:

DATE

What we did:

What we want to remember:

DATE

What we did:

What we want to remember:

Shared reflections

Something we loved making this holiday season:

A simple thing that felt surprisingly important to us:

A moment when we felt especially surrounded by love:

Something we want to try to make room for in the new year:

Highlights

These were some of the season's brightest moments:

...joy is never tomorrow;
it is always now.

SRI SRI RAVI SHANKAR

YEAR:

THIS HOLIDAY SEASON

Our special events, outings, gatherings & celebrations

DATE

What we did:

What we want to remember:

DATE

What we did:

What we want to remember:

DATE

What we did:

What we want to remember:

DATE

What we did:

What we want to remember:

Shared reflections

A moment that reminded us what the spirit of the season is all about:

A little thing someone did that meant a lot to us:

Something from the past that feels especially meaningful:

Some ways we want to cultivate togetherness in the new year:

Highlights

These were some of the season's brightest moments:

There is magic in paying attention to each other.

There is magic in giving, and magic in receiving.

The beauty of the season is its generosity... and the beauty is in our connecting.

Gratitude is when memory is stored in the heart...

LIONEL HAMPTON

YEAR:

THIS HOLIDAY SEASON

Our special events, outings, gatherings & celebrations

DATE

What we did:

What we want to remember:

DATE

What we did:

What we want to remember:

DATE

What we did:

What we want to remember:

DATE

What we did:

What we want to remember:

Shared reflections

An old memory we've been thinking a lot about:

A miracle (of any size) that warmed our hearts:

Something we rekindled an appreciation for this holiday:

Something we want to make more time for in the coming year:

Highlights

These were some of the season's brightest moments:

The miracle is this: the more we share, the more we have.

LEONARD NIMOY

YEAR:

THIS HOLIDAY SEASON

Our special events, outings, gatherings & celebrations

DATE

What we did:

What we want to remember:

DATE

What we did:

What we want to remember:

DATE

What we did:

What we want to remember:

DATE

What we did:

What we want to remember:

Shared reflections

A particularly sparkling memory from our season:

Some significant things that were given this year:

Some significant things that were received this year:

A way we're thinking about incorporating the spirit of holiday generosity into our ordinary lives:

Highlights

These were some of the season's brightest moments:

Truly happy memories always live on, shining.

BANANA YOSHIMOTO

YEAR:

THIS HOLIDAY SEASON

Our special events, outings, gatherings & celebrations

DATE

What we did:

What we want to remember:

DATE

What we did:

What we want to remember:

DATE

What we did:

What we want to remember:

DATE

What we did:

What we want to remember:

Shared reflections

Something from our history that feels especially important this holiday:

Someone who feels very much in our hearts this year:

A little but perfect moment we want to hold close:

A person or group of people we want to be more connected with in the coming year:

Highlights

These were some of the season's brightest moments:

You have to believe the magic to see it.

GUILLERMO DEL TORO

YEAR:

THIS HOLIDAY SEASON

Our special events, outings, gatherings & celebrations

DATE

What we did:

What we want to remember:

DATE

What we did:

What we want to remember:

DATE

What we did:

What we want to remember:

DATE

What we did:

What we want to remember:

Shared reflections

This was a particularly magical holiday moment:

A surprise that truly delighted us:

Some ways the holidays brought out the best in us this year:

Some ways we want to bring more joy into our new year:

Highlights

These were some of the season's brightest moments:

This holiday, may our hearts delight in the fullness of what is.

May we recognize the abundance that is all around us.

May we take none of it for granted.

When love and compassion fills your heart... life becomes a celebration.

MATA AMRITANANDAMAYI

YEAR:

THIS HOLIDAY SEASON

Our special events, outings, gatherings & celebrations

DATE

What we did:

What we want to remember:

DATE

What we did:

What we want to remember:

DATE

What we did:

What we want to remember:

DATE

What we did:

What we want to remember:

Shared reflections

A person or organization we gave a little extra to this year:

Something we felt especially appreciative of this year:

This season, we remembered the importance of:

Something we want to start doing more often—not just on holidays:

Highlights

These were some of the season's brightest moments:

...the simplest things...
give off the greatest
glow of happiness.

BOB HOPE

YEAR:

THIS HOLIDAY SEASON

Our special events, outings, gatherings & celebrations

DATE

What we did:

What we want to remember:

DATE

What we did:

What we want to remember:

DATE

What we did:

What we want to remember:

DATE

What we did:

What we want to remember:

Shared reflections

A little gift that took on big significance:

Something we did together that was a high point of the season:

A special unexpected visit, card, email, or phone call:

Some simple things we hope the new year is filled with:

Highlights

These were some of the season's brightest moments:

We are made for goodness. We are made for love... We are made for togetherness.

DESMOND TUTU

YEAR:

THIS HOLIDAY SEASON

Our special events, outings, gatherings & celebrations

DATE

What we did:

What we want to remember:

DATE

What we did:

What we want to remember:

DATE

What we did:

What we want to remember:

DATE

What we did:

What we want to remember:

Shared reflections

A day of togetherness that was especially meaningful:

We felt the presence of past generations when:

Something unique about us and the way we celebrate that we want to commemorate here:

In the coming year, we want to focus on love by:

Highlights

These were some of the season's brightest moments:

We must try
to contribute
joy to the
world.

ROGER EBERT

YEAR:

THIS HOLIDAY SEASON

Our special events, outings, gatherings & celebrations

DATE

What we did:

What we want to remember:

DATE

What we did:

What we want to remember:

DATE

What we did:

What we want to remember:

DATE

What we did:

What we want to remember:

Shared reflections

A wish that came true this holiday:

This was a moment of deep joy:

Some of the special things we made this season:

Some words or themes we want to focus on in the coming year:

Highlights

These were some of the season's brightest moments:

What shines
brightest in this season
is the best of who we are.

May our generosity
light the lives of others.

May our loved ones
feel it, near
and far.

...we should celebrate
every moment.

PAULO COELHO

YEAR:

THIS HOLIDAY SEASON

Our special events, outings, gatherings & celebrations

DATE

What we did:

What we want to remember:

DATE

What we did:

What we want to remember:

DATE

What we did:

What we want to remember:

DATE

What we did:

What we want to remember:

Shared reflections

A moment when the spirit of the season felt bright:

This season, we are feeling deeply grateful for:

Something new we discovered or enjoyed this year:

In the coming year, these are some ordinary things we want to celebrate:

Highlights

These were some of the season's brightest moments:

...it's not how much we give, but how much love we put in the giving.

MOTHER TERESA

YEAR:

THIS HOLIDAY SEASON

Our special events, outings, gatherings & celebrations

DATE

What we did:

What we want to remember:

DATE

What we did:

What we want to remember:

DATE

What we did:

What we want to remember:

DATE

What we did:

What we want to remember:

Shared reflections

A moment of holiday generosity we want to remember:

A particularly caring moment or gesture that warmed our hearts:

Someone who especially deserves our appreciation this holiday:

In the new year, these are some people or organizations we want to support:

Highlights

These were some of the season's brightest moments:

...shining moments...
are what eternity
is made of...

FRED ROGERS

YEAR:

THIS HOLIDAY SEASON

Our special events, outings, gatherings & celebrations

DATE

What we did:

What we want to remember:

DATE

What we did:

What we want to remember:

DATE

What we did:

What we want to remember:

DATE

What we did:

What we want to remember:

Shared reflections

A few seasonal smells, tastes, sights, or sounds we savored:

Something wonderful and unexpected that happened:

Something we did that felt particularly important this holiday:

In the coming year, we are especially looking forward to these things:

Highlights

These were some of the season's brightest moments:

Once in a while, when everything is just right, there is a moment of magic.

SARAH CALDWELL

YEAR:

THIS HOLIDAY SEASON

Our special events, outings, gatherings & celebrations

DATE

What we did:

What we want to remember:

DATE

What we did:

What we want to remember:

DATE

What we did:

What we want to remember:

DATE

What we did:

What we want to remember:

Shared reflections

Something truly special we received this holiday:

A moment when we felt the presence of awe or wonder:

Something that felt uniquely significant or meaningful to us this season:

We hope that the new year is filled with more of this:

Highlights

These were some of the season's brightest moments:

Let this season rekindle our gratitude for so many things: for each other, for togetherness, for the spirit of celebration, for every single giver and every single gift.

Peace is
our gift to
each other.

ELIE WIESEL

YEAR:

THIS HOLIDAY SEASON

Our special events, outings, gatherings & celebrations

DATE

What we did:

What we want to remember:

DATE

What we did:

What we want to remember:

DATE

What we did:

What we want to remember:

DATE

What we did:

What we want to remember:

Shared reflections

Something we found particular beauty in this holiday:

An especially peaceful moment we want to remember:

A movie, song, or story that had a lot of significance:

These are some ways we want to create or make room for peace in the new year:

Highlights

These were some of the season's brightest moments:

...above all,
love is a
sharing.

JAMES DILLET FREEMAN

YEAR:

THIS HOLIDAY SEASON

Our special events, outings, gatherings & celebrations

DATE

What we did:

What we want to remember:

DATE

What we did:

What we want to remember:

DATE

What we did:

What we want to remember:

DATE

What we did:

What we want to remember:

Shared reflections

This was an important thing we learned or discovered together this year:

Something we had a lot of fun giving away this holiday:

Something we had a lot of fun receiving this holiday:

In the new year, these are some people we want to spend more time with:

Highlights

These were some of the season's brightest moments:

Blessings brighten
when we count them.

MALTBIE DAVENPORT BABCOCK

YEAR:

THIS HOLIDAY SEASON

Our special events, outings, gatherings & celebrations

DATE

What we did:

What we want to remember:

DATE

What we did:

What we want to remember:

DATE

What we did:

What we want to remember:

DATE

What we did:

What we want to remember:

Shared reflections

Some things we tend to take for granted that deserve our recognition:

A person who impacted us deeply this season:

A list of little things that warmed our hearts this holiday:

Some wonderful things we already know the new year will contain:

Highlights

These were some of the season's brightest moments:

It is when you
give of yourself
that you truly give.

KAHLIL GIBRAN

YEAR:

THIS HOLIDAY SEASON

Our special events, outings, gatherings & celebrations

DATE

What we did:

What we want to remember:

DATE

What we did:

What we want to remember:

DATE

What we did:

What we want to remember:

DATE

What we did:

What we want to remember:

Shared reflections

A meaningful exchange we had this holiday:

We truly felt the spirit of the season when:

Some little gestures we found particular joy in:

In the new year, we want to give our time, skills, or resources to:

Highlights

These were some of the season's brightest moments:

May the spirit of joy
find us everywhere
this holiday.

May we treasure it
and share it with
those we meet
along the way.

How We Like to Celebrate

In our family, no holiday is complete without:

Some special things about our festivities include:

These are some of the ways we like to decorate:

This is a favorite recipe we always have to make:

INGREDIENTS:

DIRECTIONS:

Two Decades of People and Places

Looking back over the last twenty years, these are some of the people who have been the biggest part of our celebrations:

NAME: ______________________________

Why they're so important to us:

____

____

NAME: ______________________________

Why they're so important to us:

____

____

NAME: ______________________________

Why they're so important to us:

____

____

NAME: ______________________________

Why they're so important to us:

____

____

These are some of the places that have made our holidays so bright:

PLACE: ______________________________

What it means to us:

____

____

PLACE: ______________________________

What it means to us:

____

____

PLACE: ______________________________

What it means to us:

____

____

PLACE: ______________________________

What it means to us:

____

____

Two Decades of Holidays

Looking back, these are some of the most memorable holiday moments of the last twenty years:

These are some of the changes that our hearts are most deeply conscious of:

COMPENDIUM®
live inspired

Written and Compiled by: M.H. Clark
Designed by: Jessica Phoenix
Edited by: Bailey Vega

ISBN: 978-1-957891-32-3

1st printing. Printed in China with soy and metallic inks on FSC®-Mix certified paper.

Create meaningful moments with gifts that inspire.

CONNECT WITH US

live-inspired.com | sayhello@compendiuminc.com

@compendiumliveinspired
#compendiumliveinspired